TARIQ ALI and HOWARD BRENTON

IRANIAN NIGHTS

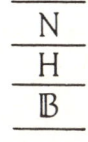

N H B

A Royal Court Programme/Text published by

NICK HERN BOOKS

A division of Walker Books Ltd

A Nick Hern Book

Iranian Nights first published in 1989 as an original paperback by Nick Hern Books, a division of Walker Books Limited, 87 Vauxhall Walk, London SE11 5HJ.
Reprinted 1989

Iranian Nights Copyright © 1989 by Tariq Ali and Howard Brenton
Introduction copyright © 1989 by Howard Brenton
Article: *The Satanic Versus the Divine* copyright © 1989 by Tariq Ali

British Library Cataloguing in Publication Data

   Tariq Ali, *1943-*
   Iranian nights
   I. Title II. Brenton, Howard, *1942-*
   822'.914

ISBN 1 85459 026 X

Caution
All rights whatsoever in this play are strictly reserved. Requests to reproduce the text in whole or in part should be addressed to the publisher. Application for performance in any medium or for translation into any language should be made to Margaret Ramsay Limited, 14a Goodwin's Court, St Martin's Lane, London WC2 4LL.

This book is sold subject to the condition that it shall not, by way of trade or otherwise, be lent, resold, hired out, or otherwise circulated without the publisher's consent in any form of binding or cover other than that in which it is published and without a similar condition including this condition being imposed on the subsequent purchaser.

Bandung Productions
in association with
The Royal Court Theatre
presents

IRANIAN NIGHTS

by

TARIQ ALI and HOWARD BRENTON

THE CALIPH	Nabil Shaban
SCHEHEREZADE	Fiona Victory
OMAR KHAYYAM	Paul Bhattacharjee

Directed by	Penny Cherns
Designed by	Colin Piggott
Costume Design	Chrissy Robinson
Lighting Design	Christopher Toulmin
Sound Design	Bryan Bowen
Stage Management	Juliet Ramsey
	Andy Pryor

The play was first performed on 19th April 1989 and runs for approximately 45 minutes without an interval

FOR THE ROYAL COURT

Artistic Director	Max Stafford-Clark
Deputy Director	Simon Curtis
General Manager	Graham Cowley
Literary Manager	Kate Harwood
Casting Director	Lisa Makin
Marketing Manager	Guy Chapman
Production Manager	Bo Barton

FOR BANDUNG PRODUCTIONS

Tariq Ali
Shirley Escott
Alistair Fraser

Press Office 01-730 2652

'When oppression exists, even the bird dies in the nest'

MOHAMMED

A NOTE

At going to press, Tariq Ali is, briefly, in Pakistan. We wrote this play together quickly, in five exciting days in a dressing room at the Royal Court Theatre amongst the make-up, flowers and first night cards of the actors performing at the theatre in the evening. Our apologies to them for the screwed-up rejected pages and full ashtrays in their workspace. The text is now being rushed by Nick Hern Books to the printer. So, dear reader, since I am 'minding the shop' for these few days while Tariq is away and the telephone link to Lahore is not ideal for writing collaborative prose, this note from half of the authorship team will have to do.

This speed is essential, because our little play is, obviously, a response to the crisis in this country generated by the appalling predicament that our brother author, Salman Rushdie, finds himself in.

We send him our solidarity and our love.

It is also obvious, from a glance at our text, that the play is not about Rushdie and his troubles, nor is it about his book, with which, if the author were with us, we would have much to quarrel.

And, for all we know, Rushdie may well, in turn, take issue with the play, should it reach him in his underground nuclear fall-out shelter, or wherever he is holed-up.

If he does, fine.

This play expounds the views of Tariq and myself, we alone are responsible for them.

For IRANIAN NIGHTS is a modest exercise in the right of free expression, in what has become something like a climate of fear. Bookshops are frightened to display or even sell SATANIC VERSES. Once rock-solid minds have crumbled in the press, with all kinds of specious arguments for banning the book, or for the cessation of its publication. Critics are afraid to appear on TV Arts shows. The Labour Party cancelled a debate in the House of Lords on a motion in support of Rushdie, under pressure from the Foreign Office. Some people I know are even afraid to read the bloody book on the underground, presumably in fear of marauding hit squads from Tehran patrolling the circle line. A little touch of fear, and fine minds seem to have gone to pieces. To quote Auden, over SATANIC VERSES it seems that

> 'Intellectual disgrace
> Stares from every human face.'

And, in the past few weeks, a silence has fallen. People are tired of the matter. England, where we boast of 'free speech', seems to have decided to let Salman Rushdie rot, and to forget him.

This must all stop. And stop now. For myself, I cannot believe this is happening in my country. It sickens me to my soul.

If the issues thrown up by this affair are not resolved, if the air is not cleared, we will have a cultural and racial crisis in our hands which will poison our national life for decades.

And . . . in the face of that danger, what can a short play do, on for nine nights in a tiny theatre and for an hour on television (we hope: on going to press, a contract with Channel Four is about to be signed . . .)?

Well, it may be very little, but perhaps it can be a pinprick for free speech?

A pinprick . . . for the richness and variety of Islamic culture and its human subtlety, and against the deathly fanaticism of the fundamentalist mullahs . . . a pinprick, for tolerance and for the Asian community, itself struggling to deal with the excesses of fundamentalism, and against the danger of white 'backlash' racism . . . a pinprick, against the cravenness of the Labour Party and the liberal critics who should both know and do better and sort their minds out . . . a pinprick, to set debate going with some humour, in a play written quickly, but, we do assure you, with minds much concentrated by the fearsome issues at stake . . . a pinprick to clear the air.

Howard Brenton
28 March 1989

Darkness. The cry of the muezzin calling the faithful to prayer.

Footsteps.

OMAR KHAYYAM *approaches. He eyes the audience.*

OMAR

In nineteen hundred and ten, in the town of Tabriz in Persia, a young Mullah stood on the roof terrace of his house and looked at the sky and saw Halley's comet. His name was Ahmad Kasravi. Halley's comet was passing over Persia that night. Kasravi saw the comet. The 'Star With A Tail' seduced him away from the true path. The godless science of Europe infected his mind. He became a heretic, a Mullah turned inside out. In the language of learning, Arabic, the language of our Prophet (peace be upon him), he wrote books. Books which tore at the faith of the Imams. In nineteen hundred and forty-six . . .

CALIPH

(*Interrupting.*)
Dog! Hast thou forgotten thine own calendar?

OMAR

In thirteen hundred and sixteen Kasravi the unbeliever was brought to trial on the charge of slandering Islam. The Devotees did not wait for the verdict. They shot him in open court. Once death is decreed, God's will be done. So perish the enemies of our faith. So perish apostates. So perish their supporters.

He points at the audience. Then smiles and sniffs.

Strong stuff, eh? Don't worry, it's not mine. I'm just a poet, earning a crust. My name's Omar Khayyam. This is me . . .

> The Moving Finger writes; and, having writ,
> Moves on: nor all thy Piety nor Wit
>   Shall lure it back to cancel half a Line,
> Nor all thy tears wash out a Word of it.
>
> . . . Ah, Love! could thou and I with fate conspire
> To grasp this sorry Scheme of Things entire,
>   Would not we shatter it to bits – and
> Re-mould it near to the Heart's Desire!

Dodgy, very dodgy. Poems and stories. Endless trouble. Witness her predicament. Scheherezade before the Caliph.

He found his wife in bed with a slave. Chopped her head off. Been revenging himself against women ever since. Fuck a virgin every night and have her killed, so no one else can do the same. This one's survived, a young white slave girl. Has to keep a drowsy Emperor awake, a good story a night or else.

OMAR makes a throat-cutting sign.

It's not just Sinbad or Ali Baba. Scheherezade tells stories which sends a pringle down your dingle. The crown jewels of Arabian literature, the *One Thousand and One Nights*.

The CALIPH drinks wine. He slobbers.
SCHEHEREZADE crawls to him and wipes his face clean.

CALIPH
(*Shouts.*)

Number of tonight's story!

OMAR
Eight hundred and seventy-three my Lord!

CALIPH
Is it moral?

OMAR
Highly, my Lord.

CALIPH
(*Enraged.*)

No more morals. Too many mullahs, too many morals. Tell me about wine.

SCHEHEREZADE
How can we talk about wine, when the body is so explicit on the subject? It is forbidden, my Lord.

CALIPH
What about copulation then?

She looks down modestly.

OMAR
(*Aside.*)

No population without copulation, no copulation without population.

He frowns.

SCHEHEREZADE
Copulation is that act which unites the sexes of man and woman. It is an excellent thing. It lightens the body and relieves the soul. It cures melancholy, tempers the heat of passion, contents the heart. All complete copulation is followed by moisture. In the woman this moisture is produced by the emotion felt in her honourable parts; in the man, by the running of that sap which is secreted by the two eggs. This sap follows a complicated road; man possesses one large vein which gives birth to all other veins; the blood which fortifies these three hundred and sixty smaller veins runs at last into a tube which debouches in the left egg; in this egg the blood turns about, clarifies, and changes into a white liquid which thickens because of the heat of the egg, and smells like palm milk.

CALIPH
Enough enough. Arouse me not, it is not to my convenience. Something moral, after all.

OMAR
What about this, my Lord:

(Sings.)
Lust is not content with blushes
Kisses taken from pure lips,
Not content with wedded glances:
Lust must have a thing which dances,
Lust must have a thing which gushes
Lust must have a thing which drips.

CALIPH
Obscure nonsense. Scheherezade, we are still waiting.

OMAR
Story eight hundred and seventy-four.

SCHEHEREZADE
There was once an Emperor of Persia, tyrant and torturer, beloved of Satan. Satan gave him all his heart desired. Three million swords, a million crossbows and twenty-eight cadillacs. In return Satan wanted an oil monopoly.

The CALIPH *nods knowingly.*

The Emperor said yes. The people said no. Persia became a prison. In a far off land a Holy Man saw all this and rose with wrath. He told his priests, 'Tear down his palace, break his swords, steal his crossbows and hide his cadillacs.'

CALIPH

Hmm. Very wise. Hmm.

OMAR
(*Aside.*)

Prison doors were opened. Prisoners left. Prisoners returned. Prison doors were shut.

SCHEHEREZADE

Satan spoke words of anger and rage. But whispered: 'All are corrupt. One day this Holy Man, too, will be mine.' And the Holy Man grew old, wars engulfed the land near to ruin. Believer fought against believer. The fountains ran with blood. A million believers died. The war lost, the Holy Man looked up from his bed of pain. He sought a cause to unite his people once again.

The CALIPH *sits up.*

From far away a messenger came with evil news. On a small island in Satan's thrall, where two Queens sat on a single throne, a poet from an old family of believers in the East had written a poem. The blasphemous wretch.

CALIPH

Ah. Theology. Heads will roll. And what was the blasphemy?

SCHEHEREZADE

No one knows. It was a book that nobody could read. Without further thought, the Holy Man said, 'Bring me this poet's head.' The little island trembled. Fear stalked its book markets. 'Til one day the poet said, I will go and meet the Holy Man armed only with my thoughts and verses, and sewn into my coat, that book which no one can read.

CALIPH
(*Rising.*)

I think I will play the Holy Man. Are the executioners ready?

OMAR

They're all on strike.

CALIPH
(*As he becomes the* HOLY MAN, *putting the robe on, helped by* SCHEHEREZADE, *who gives his behind a little rub.*)

Have them shot.

OMAR
(*Aside.*)

Who will execute the executioners?

SCHEHEREZADE
(*Aside.*)

Who will educate the educated?

War music.

OMAR *as* POET
(*He carries a blown up Penguin. He talks to it.*)

I journey to Persia. Through marshes thick with corpses. Past burnt out chariots, the air fouled by enemy vapours. Everywhere the smell of war. Is this the land of the pure? I come to the city where seminaries abound, where crowds pray and shout for vengeance. These verses sewn into my coat weigh me down. I'm scared.

The Holy Man and the Poet

CALIPH *as* HOLY MAN

Execute that Penguin.

SCHEHEREZADE *pricks the Penguin with a large stiletto.*

POET *and* HOLY MAN *stare at each other. A silence.*

HOLY MAN
I can do nothing for you. I am a simple human being.
It is God who has spoken.

SCHEHEREZADE
And the Poet tried to remember all the clever things his friends had said to him, at dinner parties on the Island in Satan's thrall.

POET
Heresy! Holy Man, are your words the same as God's?

HOLY MAN
Be calm. Your death is assured.

POET
If I have truly offended, I apologise. That was not my intent. I too am just a human being. For all I know, it was Satan himself who planted these verses in my head.

HOLY MAN
Apostate! Do you turn to mockery now?

SCHEHEREZADE
And the Holy Man rose in anger. Hear his true words of wisdom, and tremble.

HOLY MAN
Those who follow the West imagine that the Islamic precepts are harsh. These people do not know what these precepts are for. It is like a physician who holds the knife and tears the abdomen in order to remove a cancer, and someone says, 'The physician is harsh.' The physician who cuts off a hand, does it because that hand will putrify the human body. Society is like the human body and sometimes, for rectifying a society, it will punish a person, punishment that on occasion results in his killing. One who corrupts a country, or a group, and is incorrigible, he must be eliminated for the sake of purifying and protecting the society; this cancerous gland must be removed from the society and its removal is done by executing him. Such are Islamic executions. Islamic executions are bountiful executions.

POET
Look, do you mind if I smoke?

The HOLY MAN *stares.*

I will, surely, smoke for ever in Hell?

The HOLY MAN *stares. The* POET *does not smoke.*

HOLY MAN
You have lived in the West too long. You no longer understand that truth is encompassed in one sentence. 'There is only one God, and Mohammed is his prophet.'

POET
Look here, let's debate this. Let us raise this, say, to the level of The House of Commons. My point is, there's nothing original in what you're saying. Every great religion has been through this. The Catholic Inquisition accused Galileo Galilei of abolishing Heaven, when all he said was that the Earth went round the Sun. The Jewish elders excommunicated their

greatest philosopher, Spinoza, when all he did was pull the wings off flies to see if God would intervene; the Protestant Church was thunderstruck when Darwin abolished Adam and Eve. They have survived and become more human. Why are you holding Islam back? There is enough wealth. Why is your country not the Islamic Heaven on earth?

HOLY MAN

Every religion that travelled to the West was tainted; dissipated into a Satanic mire of self-indulgence, wordly illusion. I am not ignorant. Why didn't you write a *good* poem that everyone could read, you know, something like Tom Brown's School Days. It might have saved your life.

POET

What madness have my verses unleashed? A fiction greater than any poet's imagination. Now jokes become daggers and rhymes become bullets. In the name of God, the Compassionate, the Merciful, the Benificent.

HOLY MAN

You will die. It is God's will.

POET

In Heaven's name, why?

HOLY MAN

Either choose not to make friends with elephant drivers or build a house fit for an elephant.

POET

What?

A pause.

Right. Right. Let's get this on a rational level. I'll ask you some questions. If your answers convince me, I will go down on my knees, in shame, I'll pray for forgiveness, plead for mercy, commit myself to a pious life and burn my verses that no one can read.

The HOLY MAN *stares impassively, no trace of emotion on his face.*

Is it or is it not the case, that the Prophet explicitly forbad the creation of a clergy?

To these questions, every time there is no reply.

In the war of believer against believer, with your twelve year-olds dead in the marshes, which . . . side . . . did . . . God . . . support?

Silence.

You said that the man who will kill me, will go to Heaven. How ... do ... you ... know? Is it not the case, that God alone decides who goes to Heaven or to Hell?

Silence.

Why is it that all your wars are fought against other believers?

Silence.

Why do you not seek to convert me? Can you only spread the name of God by chopping off heads?

Silence.

At the time of the Prophet's birth, was his mother a Muslim?

Silence.

And if you had lived at the time of the Prophet, when do you think you would have become a believer?

Silence.

In your last exile, which Muslim city gave you refuge?

Silence.

Do your threats actually have anything ... to ... do ... with Islam? Or is it just the same old story, power, terror and Realpolitik?

A silence.

And are you sure that you yourself will go to Heaven?

SCHEHEREZADE

The Holy Man did not answer. Not because he did not have his answers, but because he saw no point in answering a dead man on leave. Not that the poet had asked all the questions. He did not ask the Holy Man why, in his land, dissident women in prison who were virgins had to be raped because the Holy Man's jailers believed that virgins who die go straight to Heaven.

CALIPH

Stop, this weighs upon my heart. There's only one moral in your story. That the tongue of every poet should be plucked out at birth. Give us quick stories, quickly.

OMAR

Story number eight seven six.

SCHEHEREZADE
There was once a blind poet in the old town of Ma'arra.

The CALIPH *frowns.*

He once wrote:

OMAR
(*Recites.*)
The inhabitants of the earth are of two sorts
  Those with brains but no religion,
And those with religion but no brains.

CALIPH
(*Interrupting.*)
Stop! I said no more poets.

OMAR
Story eight seven seven.

SCHEHEREZADE
A great Sultan went to rest one noon in the bedchamber of his Queen and was stretching himself on the bed, when he noticed in the middle of it a large and quite fresh stain, the origin of which there could be no mistake.

The world darkened before his eyes. Tottering with indignation, he sought out his Queen. Eyes on fire and beard trembling, he said to her: 'What is this stain on our bed?'

The Queen bent, sniffed the stain and pronounced, 'It is man's semen, O Commander of the Faithful.'

'I have not lain with you for a month, can you explain its presence?'

'Can you possibly suspect me of fornication, my Lord?' exclaimed the Queen.

'Yes! Let the Kadi, judge of our faith, determine whether you are guilty or innocent.'

The Kadi came, sniffed the stain and found himself in a difficult position. A wrong word and the Queen's head was gone. In order to gain time, he looked up at the ceiling and saw the wing of a bat, extruding from a hole in which it was sleeping. He grabbed a lance and stabbed the bat, which fell to the bed. Then he said:

'O Commander of the Faithful, the books of medicine teach us that the bat's semen closely resembles that of a man. The mess was certainly made by this bat while he looked down upon our Lady Queen in her sleep. You see that I have punished his lust with death.'

Laughter.

CALIPH
Too close to the Imperial bone. Now, clean the air. Now, remind me of the sayings of the Prophet.

OMAR
(Formally.)
Sayings of our Holy Prophet Mohammed (may peace be upon him).

SCHEHEREZADE
When oppression exists, even the bird dies in its nest.

A silence.

OMAR
I order you to assist any oppressed person, whether he is a Muslim or not.

CALIPH
Trust in God, but tie your camel first.

SCHEHEREZADE
No monkery in Islam.

OMAR
Whoever has no kindness, has no faith.

CALIPH
In some poetry there is wisdom.

SCHEHEREZADE
Women are the twin halves of men.

OMAR
Speaking the truth to the unjust is the best of holy wars.

SCHEHEREZADE
A man slips with his tongue more than with his feet.

OMAR
The ink of the learned is holier than the blood of the martyr.

The Transformation of the Caliph

CALIPH

Oh but I weary
   Of my tyranny
Forcing this woman to sing to me

I weary of holy purity
   In a land of Third World poverty –
I'll go to the West and be free

Yes! I'll join the immigrants
   I'll put on Western pants
I'll enter England illegally

I'll no longer be a king
   I'll have nothing
Nothing at all, I'll be

An Easterner in the West –
   I'll sweat, I'll save, I'll do my best
As Americans say, suck it and see

I'll live in Bradford, Yorkshire
   I'll drink a lot of English beer
And I will raise a family

Of heroic sons, proud of me
   Free of prejudice, free of poverty
True sons of liberty.

The CALIPH *as* FATHER. OMAR *as the* SON.

SCHEHEREZADE

He came in '58. Moved up North. Worked on the buses. Punched tickets at railway stations. A decent man. Enjoyed his beer and said his prayers. Then he moved his family here, his wife and two sons, aged three and four, whom he loved. They missed the sun.

But to his joy the older one loved his school, made new friends, played cricket, had fun. The father worked hard, saved money, the mother complained. She hated Yorkshire pudding and the rain. To make her happy he opened a restaurant, he called it 'The Joy of Gurkha', because he knew the Brits loved Gurkhas.

His wildest dream came true. The older boy, brilliant at maths, went to King's College Cambridge.

But something happened there, no one knows why, the son lost his way. Forgot his maths. Sold his books. Forced his English girlfriend to convert to Islam, then threw her out and grew a beard.

The FATHER *in shabby restaurateur's clothes, apron, holding up a brass tray of pickles. The* SON *in fashionable business suit, with a beard.*

SON

Don't mock the Party of Islam, Father! In this town alone we have three hundred members and two thousand sympathisers. Already they fear us. I know you are angry, but please understand.

FATHER

My son, I am ashamed when I see you on television burning books. I grew up in Mirpur, illiterate, unread, desperate for knowledge. I worked fourteen hours a day, and many nights, to give you something I never had. So proud, at school your teacher said 'Your boy is brilliant at maths', so proud when you got your scholarship to Cambridge. Even when you said, 'Father do not come to Cambridge', I understood. I did not want to embarrass you. I gave you the key to an enlightened world, you have thrown it away. And now you shout and scream murder and death and 'Kill the poet.'

SON

I never told you what happened at Cambridge. I did not want you and mother upset, I did not want you to feel it was all in vain. I was out one night with Julia. Walking. The Boat Club were celebrating, drunk, crazed, vomiting, immaculately dressed, the English upper-classes at their best. They saw me across the street. They chased me, shouting 'Get the wog.' Julia screamed and ran for help that never arrived. They dragged me into a college quad. I did not resist, there were six of them. They stripped me naked, they spat, they kicked my balls, called me a circumcised pig, 'Hey this wog is a Jew' someone said, and then one of them bent over and shat on my head. They left me shivering. I wept that night, father, I cried and cried. That night I swore I never would be humiliated again. I found myself reciting the creed of my faith.

FATHER

Why did you not tell me this?

SON

You sent me there, father. How could I think about Bertrand Russell or Wittgenstein? I had no identity. I was a shivering stranger, beaten and battered. Those verses, learnt parrot-like when I was a child, now blazed with fire. I threw their books in a college dustbin, and turned to ours. I read the life of the Prophet. I read the Holy Book. And I have come to this revelation. This country can be saved. We mustn't despair. These Islands must convert to Islam. Their religion is dead. Atrophied. Corrupt. Only a Godless religion could make a woman a priest.

FATHER
(Recovering from his shock.)

Do you really mean . . . That Prince Philip will grow a Muslim's beard? That Princess Di and Margaret Thatcher will take the veil? That the Archbishop of Canterbury will climb on top of his cathedral and call the faithful to prayer? That Ian Paisley will bow before Mecca five times a day? That Mr Haig in Scotland will pour his whisky into the North Sea? Do you think that Mr Marmaduke Hussey of the BBC will change his name to Mahmud Hussein and broadcast Friday prayers live from Wembley Stadium? Do you think Mr Roy Hattersley will agree to be flogged in public for drinking? And when you've closed down the brothels and casinos in Mayfair, you bloody fool, where do you think the leaders of our Muslim world will go?

Convert this country to Islam? Are you mad? It would be far easier for Mr Rupert Murdoch to become a citizen of Iran, than for this country to convert to Islam.

I don't like the pretence behind your beard. I don't believe you. I too have been spat on and abused. It did not turn me inside out.

SON

Careful father, you stand on the frontiers of apostasy. I learnt my religion on your knee. God forbid that I have to stone your restaurant. Can't you see you've failed? Five years a Labour Councillor. Result, nothing. Fifteen years Chairman of Multicultural Committee for Racial Integration. Result, nothing. Friendly drinks at the pub. Result, nothing. Don't think I don't know where you go on Saturday nights.

FATHER

Bastard.

SON
Nothing. You're nothing, nothing. You've forgotten who you are.

FATHER
You don't know who I am. You don't know who I was. It makes me sad to see you drift into unreality. Listen, boy. The world I came from was the world of a village. Yes, we were good Muslims. Yes, we prayed to our God. We did not need a Party of Islam to remind us who we were. And the mullahs. Ignorant, corrupt, hypocrites: the whole village hated them. Do you know why? The mullah in our village stole food, drank on the sly and one afternoon after prayers was seen interfering with a goat behind a bush. Don't talk to me about them.

SON
Stop. Stop. The clergy of God are covered in martyrs blood.

FATHER
God has no clergy. That is what my religion taught me.

SCHEHEREZADE
There they stood. Father and son. Father more angry than son. Son more angry than father. The father grieving. The son hating. Shocked, at a loss. Gripped by a rage beyond their control. The gulf between them grew and grew. Helpless in division they denied they were son and father.

SON
A book burns and the unbelievers run in fear.

FATHER
A book burns and we are all shamed.

SON
Our way works, old man. Three members of their Cabinet mumbled apologies. Fear makes them tremble. They cave in.

FATHER
Fear is not a weapon of God.

SON
But it works. A few threats, and the enlightenment is forgotten. Their intellectuals flop to the floor in pools of jelly. Sorry Mr Black Man, sir, we didn't mean to offend your religion, sir. Your Book is great, sir, much better than this punk poet. If we stop printing his verses will you promise to go back to your corner and do whatever it is you do with your religion? We like it really. Feel free to fly around on your magic carpet. Free speech. They cut their own tongues out. God is great! God is great!

FATHER

You talk like this and you fly on Concorde to Bahrain every week.

SON

God's work.

FATHER

God's work my arse. You're a pimp. A broker. Taking the city of London to a medieval Sheikdom. Your Islam is an old boy's network. I see it all. For you the green colour of faith is the green colour of dollars. Your party in this town is a protection racket.

SON

You have crossed the frontier. This is blasphemy. Father, change the locks on your restaurant. Put grilles on your windows and check your fire insurance.

FATHER
(*Livid.*)

Are you threatening me?

SON
(*Slyly.*)

It is God who decrees. I am just a soldier of Islam.

FATHER

Out. Out of the door. Get out. You are finished for me.

The FATHER *walks away.*

SATAN, *his voice fruity Oxbridge, City, speaks out of the air, as if on a telephone call.*

SATAN

Hello Ahmed. How are you?

SON

Very depressed. I've just broken with my father.

SATAN

Anything I can do?

SON

It's religion.

SATAN

C. of E. myself. We don't go in for religion much. Now, listen Ahmed. I want to put something your way.

SON

Shoot.

SATAN

You people seem to be doing rather well. You've even got HMG on the run. But you need a bit of help, I think. Specially if you do bump him off, ha ha ha! By the way, I know a bunch of unsavoury characters who can take care of that. At a price.

SON

It is taken care of.

SATAN

That's your affair. Couldn't get past page fifteen myself. But you do have an image problem.

SON

Islam doesn't go in for images.

A pause.

What do you have in mind?

SATAN

I'll be straight with you. My consultancy has ten per cent riding on this.

SON

I'm listening.

SATAN

It's the way your people spit in TV, in news interviews. The funny dress, too much hair. Unruly beards. Now there is a company that can sell anything. They're giving Union Carbide a friendly image in India, they've advised Boeing to construct a swimming pool in Lockerbie, they're working on getting Ghadafi on Desert Island Discs.

SON

They are an advertising agency.

SATAN

I do think God could do with it. Or your version of God. You see, now you've got everyone in the country shitting in their pants, you've got to move onto your next phase.

SON

We will kill the poet.

SATAN

Yes yes, you've done well, shut a lot of big mouths up. But, my dear Ahmed, you and I know that you've not really changed, since that dreadful incident at Cambridge. Have I ever apologised for that?

SON

Think nothing of it. Now what did you really ring me up about?

SATAN

Your people bringing the stuff in. I'm talking poppy fields here.

SON

Only alcohol is forbidden.

SATAN

Quite. The American distributors want it legit. They're looking at Islamic banks.

A silence.

Can you help?

SON

I'll fly to Florida tomorrow morning.

SATAN

Good to talk to you, Ahmed. Bye.

SON

Goodbye Satan.

The Father's Lament

FATHER

I am told that fear is spread
   That the good are beginning to get worried
And cowardice is beginning to eat the soul.

The poet's predicament
   Is now the subject
Of interminable discussions.

In chanceries
   And at dinner tables
New York Paris, London, Rome

The conversation begins to flag
   Will he live
Will he die?

Is it true that some mullahs
   Can fly?
'Only an arrogant, self-centred fool,'

Declares a Western critic,
   His way of seeing the world
Strangely altered,

'Would pit his paltry verse
   Against the genius
Of the Divine book.'

The Poet
   In his underground nuclear shelter
Chuckles sadly and thinks –

'Fascism in brown shirts
   Is evil
Everyone agrees . . .

But Fascism in brown skins
   That
The decent cannot deal with . . .

As for me
   I feel a dumb and speechless pain
I still believe

But not in the Heaven
   Of which the preachers drone
I feel alone . . . '

SCHEHEREZADE

Scheherezade has run away
   Slipped the callous
Tyrant's chains, crept

From Persia
   Now I live in Nottinghill
With my Mum

She is not well
   The terror, the fear
Have broken her –

Who can understand the fate
   Of the prisoner and the poor
Who have fled from hate

To a nowhere in the West
   A nowhere in the rain?
Who can understand our pain?

Why does the West
   Think it can do no wrong
And expect the refugee

To be superhumanly strong?
   More tolerant, more wise
Than any human being

Can be? The miracle
   Is so many of us do
Have the strength to bear the abuse

Bear the blind ignorance of what we are
   And where we come from
A miracle

That only a few have gone fanatic
   That only a few
Rave about the Satanic

Therefore the more who speak out
   The better
The more, the more the better

Of the profound
   Matter of the nature of God and man
Speak out as best you can

What finer sound
   Is there than a human being
Singing

Against
   Cruelty, against
     Hate.

Drumroll and Call

A drumroll. The actors take it in turn to call out the names of the writers.

Dante.

Drumroll.

Christopher Marlowe.

Drumroll.

Oscar Wilde.

Drumroll.

Omar Khayyam.

Drumroll.

James Joyce.

Drumroll.

Al Ma'avi.

Drumroll.

D H Lawrence.

Drumroll.

Naguib Mahfouz.

Drumroll.

Sean O'Casey.

Drumroll.

Faiz.

Drumroll.

Bertolt Brecht.

Drumroll.

Vasili Grossman.

Drumroll.

Gabriel Garcia Marquez.

Drumroll.

                            ALL THREE

Salman Rushdie!

THE SATANIC VERSUS THE DIVINE

'Manuscripts don't burn', wrote Bulgakov, the great Soviet novelist of the Twenties and Thirties, in a thinly-veiled rebuke to the Stalinist censors. But the same does not apply to a writer who is, after all, only made of bones and flesh. Messages often survive, but all messengers are mortal. What then are we to make of the grotesquely surreal scenario through which we are all living. A multiplication of tragedies is taking place.

First, of course, there is the plight of the writer. Salman Rushdie is holed up in a secure house and guarded day and night by the British security forces, an Iranian hostage on British soil. Reality, as we know, is stranger than most fiction. The scenes we are observing could easily be excerpts from a Rushdie novel. But don't be deceived. They are only too real and the novelist's life is under very serious threat. Even if he survives this crisis the spectre of death will haunt him for the rest of his life.

There is, however, an even bigger tragedy. For this whole affair has now transcended both Salman Rushdie and the 'Satanic Verses'. This is the tragedy of Islam and its place in the modern world.

When Khomeini first pronounced his death sentence, my first reaction was one of disbelief. Was it really possible that the exalted spiritual leader of Shiite Islam was publicly ordering the execution of a novelist who writes exclusively in the English language? Was it just my imagination or was it really the case that the main inspirer of the Islamic Republic was speaking in the language of a mafia godfather? The day after, another cleric decided to mimic the satanic gangsters of the United States. A price was put on Rushdie's head: three million for any Muslim who killed him and a million for anyone else. And all this in the name of Allah, the Compassionate and Merciful?

Why was money necessary in the first place? Khomeini had offered any Muslim assassin a one-way ticket to Heaven. Let us pause and reflect on this for a moment. Surely the decision on who goes to Heaven or, for that matter, to Hell rests with the Creator. How dare anyone abrogate that right? Is Imam

Khomeini now claiming to be a Prophet in direct contact with his Maker? Why don't good Muslims find Khomeini's words heretical? And, digressing slightly, is it not the case that Islam abhors priestly hierarchies and expressly forbids the creation of any ideological monopoly by the clerics? All Muslims are supposed to be equal in the sight of God. Why then these frenzied Nurnberg-style rallies in which Shiite Muslims abase themselves before a mere priest?

In fact very little of what is now taking place has all that much to do with religion. Of course there are many non-fundamentalist Muslims who have actually read the novel and find some passages offensive, but most of them would agree that the only way to combat Rushdie is through a battle of ideas. This is both legitimate and the only serious way of convincing people. Let us not forget that the first cadres of the Islamic faith were NOT won over at the point of a sword but through a process of debate and discussion.

Khomeini is utilising the hullaballoo over the SATANIC VERSES to impose a ruthlessly conformist cultural model within Islam. Stalin and his cultural commissars gave the world 'socialist realism'. Khomeini and his ideological policemen insist upon their particular brand of 'Islamic realism'. Salman Rushdie has become a convenient pretext to further this aim amongst others. The Iranian clergy have not scored any real victories against the infidels. Their wrath has been concentrated against Muslims. The Iran-Iraq war cost over a million lives on both sides. Where was Islam when this conflict was taking place? Which side did God support? And how many dissenters from within the cultural tradition of Islam have been exterminated by the zealots. Tens of thousands of political prisoners have been wiped out. Women prisoners who were virgins have been raped in prison. Why? Because virgins, say the Ayatollah's men, go straight to Heaven. Mass rape ensures an easy passage to Hell. Is this the Islam which good believers want to present to the world?

Islam has always had a tolerant side. There has been a long tradition of intellectual dissent in the Muslim world. After the Prophet's death, his youngest wife, Ayesha, actually raised the banner of revolt against the anointed successor. Disputes on the interpretation of Islam take place to this very day. The richness of early Islamic civilization has left its mark on the entire world. Culture and science owe a great deal to that old tradition. Would the *Arabian Nights*, I wonder, get a clean bill of health today from the Imam in Teheran?

In the Indian subcontinent (which produced Salman Rushdie) Islam was popularised by sufi holy men who were subsequently venerated as saints. Their ecstatic dances and existential poetry shaped Islam throughout Northern India. This was (and is) a joyous Islam which threatens nobody, which preaches an individual communion with the Great Sufi in the sky and which is, for that very reason, loathed by the puritanical preachers of fundamentalism. To this day the music influenced by the sufi tradition mocks the hypocrisy of the mullahs.

Take, for instance, the following fact. One of the instigators of the riot in Islamabad which led to the unforgiveable loss of six lives was a Maulana named Kausar Niazi. This particular Maulana, during the Sixties and Seventies, was a ferocious opponent of the Jamaat-i-Islami brand of fundamentalism. For this reason Zulfiqar Ali Bhutto hired him and made him a Cabinet Minister. He was Bhutto's weapon against the fundamentalists. Niazi, a colourful fellow, enjoyed his drink and the company of dancing girls. Bhutto's nickname for him was Maulana Whisky. Now, deprived of power and influence, old Whisky is trying to rehabilitate himself with his former enemies and pressuring Bhutto's daughter to take him seriously. What I want to know is why he waited several months after the publication of this book?

All the great Muslim poets of India have, at some time or another, questioned the practice of religion. Ghalib, Iqbal and Faiz were all embroiled in conflicts with the mullahs. When Iqbal wrote his 'Complaint to God', he was denounced by the clergy as an apostate! His message, written in his poem 'New Temple', denounced organised religion. It would be dismissed out of hand in Teheran, but Muslims in South Asia could learn a great deal from these words of the poet:

I shall tell the truth, O Brahmin, but take it not as an offence:
The idols in thy temple have decayed.
Thou hast learnt from these images to bear ill-will to thine own people;
And God has taught the Muslim preacher
the ways of strife.
My heart was sick: I turned away both from the temple and the Ka'bah;
From the sermons of the preacher and from thy fairy tales, oh Brahmin.
To thee images of stone embody the divine –
For me, every particle of my country's dust is a deity.
Come, let us remove all that causes estrangement.

Let us reconcile these that have turned away from each other,
remove all sign of division.
Desolation has reigned for long in the habitation of my
heart –
Come, let us build a new temple in our land,
Let our holy place be higher than any on the earth.
Let us raise its pinnacle till it touches the lapels of the sky;
Let us awake every morning to sing the sweetest songs,
And give worshippers the wine of love to drink.

Tariq Ali

[This article was written for the *Literary Gazette* in Moscow.]

TARIQ ALI is the author of several books on world history and politics. He is co-producer of Channel Four's *Bandung File* and has produced and scripted a feature film, *Partition*. He is currently working on his first novel.

HOWARD BRENTON is well known as a controversial playwright and has had many plays premiered by the Royal Court Theatre, the Royal Shakespeare Company and the National Theatre. Among his most famous are *The Churchill Play*, *The Romans in Britain* and *Pravda* (written with David Hare). His first novel, *Diving for Pearls*, will be published this summer.